21st Century Junior Library

DISCOVER THE GIANT GROUND SLOTH

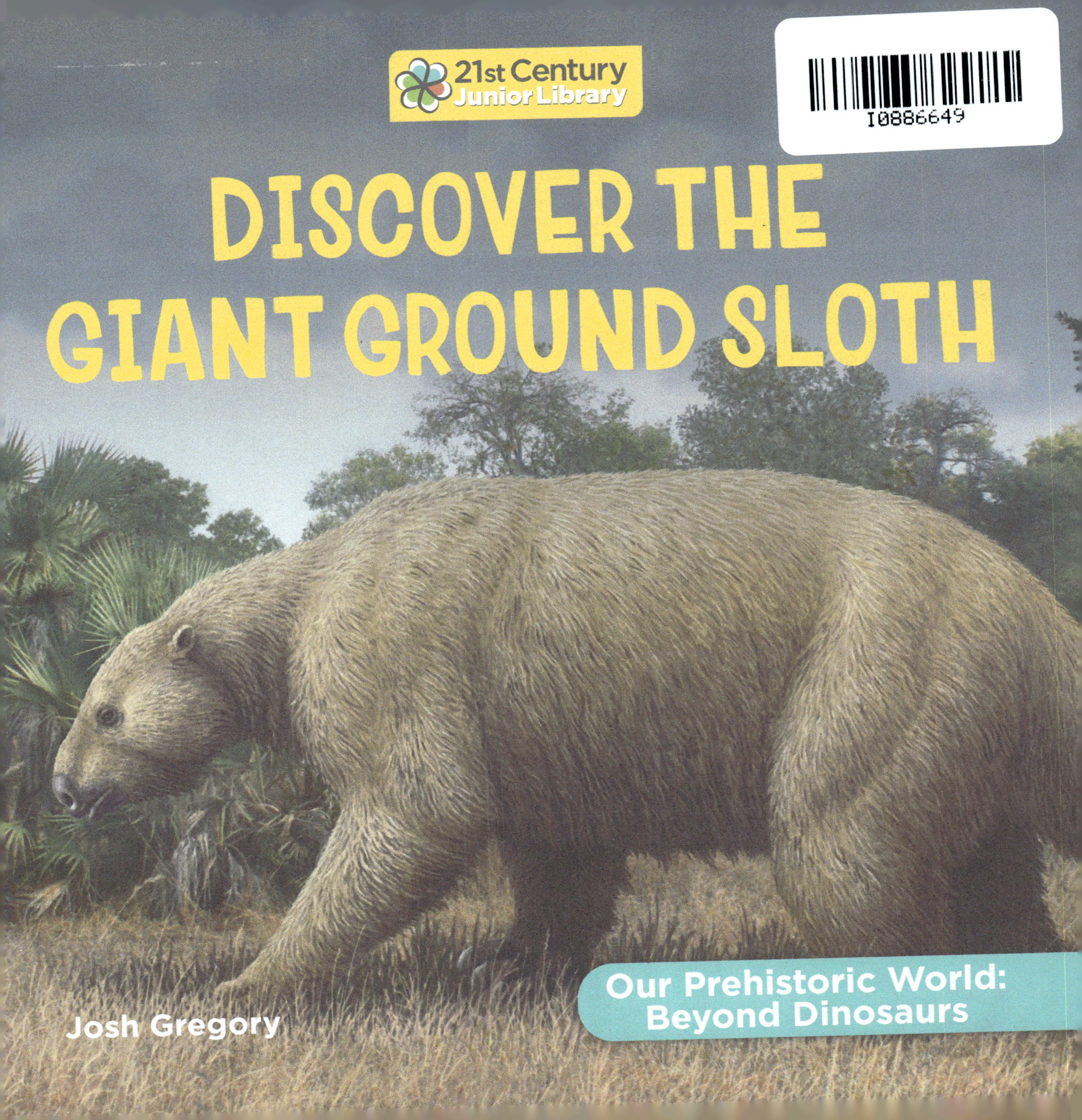

Our Prehistoric World: Beyond Dinosaurs

Josh Gregory

Published in the United States of America by:

CHERRY LAKE PRESS
2395 South Huron Parkway, Suite 200, Ann Arbor, Michigan 48104
www.cherrylakepress.com

Reading Adviser: Beth Walker Gambro, MS, Ed., Reading Consultant, Yorkville, IL

Photo and Illustration Credits: © MAURICIO ANTON/SCIENCE PHOTO LIBRARY, cover, title page; © Illustration by Brian Engh, 5; Benjamin Waterhouse Hawkins, Public domain, via Wikimedia Commons, 6; © Aunt_Spray/iStock.com, 7; © JAMES KUETHER/SCIENCE PHOTO LIBRARY, 8–9; Heinrich Harder (1858-1935), Public domain, via Wikimedia Commons, 10; © ISKGAE/Shutterstock, 11; ДиБгд, CC BY-SA 4.0 via Wikimedia Commons, 12–13; © Illustration by Brian Engh, 14; © Catmando/Shutterstock, 16–17; © ROMAN UCHYTEL/SCIENCE PHOTO LIBRARY, 18; Dallas Krentzel, CC BY 2.0 via Wikimedia Commons, 20

Cherry Lake Press is an imprint of Cherry Lake Publishing Group.

Library of Congress Cataloging-in-Publication Data has been filed and is available at catalog.loc.gov.

Cherry Lake Press would like to acknowledge the work of the Partnership for 21st Century Learning, a Network of Battelle for Kids. Please visit Battelle for Kids online for more information.

Printed in the United States of America

CHERRY LAKE PRESS

CONTENTS

WHAT WAS A GIANT GROUND SLOTH?

Have you ever seen a sloth? These animals move very slowly. They live in the rainforests of Central and South America. They hang from tree branches. Other kinds of sloths lived long ago. These sloths were much bigger than the ones that live today. They were way too big to hang from tree branches. Instead, they lived mostly on the ground.

Even though they were bigger, giant ground sloths were likely faster than modern sloths.

Many **species** of giant ground sloths roamed Earth. The earliest ones lived around 30 million years ago. The last of them went **extinct** around 5,000 years ago. At first, they lived only in South America. About 2.7 million years ago, they started moving into North America.

Glyptodons were prehistoric armadillos. They lived at the same time as giant ground sloths.

Make a Guess!

Can you imagine a giant ground sloth living in your backyard? It might have happened long ago! What else would have been different back then about the place you live?

WHAT DID A GIANT GROUND SLOTH LOOK LIKE?

Ground sloths had a lot in common with today's sloths. They were covered in shaggy fur. They had long claws and powerful legs. But they weren't just bigger versions of sloths. They had faces that made them look a little like bears. Many also had longer tails.

Why did giant ground sloths have longer tails? Scientists think the tails helped them balance when they stood on their back legs to reach food.

The biggest ground sloth species was called *Megatherium*. It weighed up to about 8,000 pounds (3,629 kilograms). That's as heavy as an adult elephant! *Megatherium* was also very tall. It could reach a height of 18 feet (5.5 meters) standing on its back legs. That's about as tall as a giraffe!

A 2025 study showed that Megatherium had a dense coat of fur. This helped keep it warm in colder climates.

Look!

Take a look at the tree sloths that live today. You can see them in zoos or in online videos. Can you imagine a sloth the size of an elephant?

Even the smallest ground sloths were still very big. One of the smallest species was the Shasta ground sloth. It weighed up to 550 pounds (250 kg). It stood up to 9 feet (2.7 m) tall. Each ground sloth species was slightly different. Some were bigger or smaller. Others had different kinds of claws or teeth.

Shasta ground sloths are named after Shasta County, California. That's where the first fossils were found.

Scientists are able to tell what ground sloths ate based on the shape of their teeth. Flat teeth could grind up plants. Sharp teeth could tear plants or meat.

HOW DID A GIANT GROUND SLOTH LIVE?

Most ground sloths were **herbivores**. Some species **grazed** on grass. Others ate leaves and fruit from trees. Certain species spent a lot of time in water. They ate seaweed and other underwater plants. Some larger ground sloths might have eaten a little meat, too. They weren't **predators**. But they wouldn't let meat go to waste if they found it.

Ground sloths likely used their front legs to hold themselves up against trees. Then they could reach the higher leaves with their tongues.

Ground sloths were too heavy to climb trees. But they were tall enough to reach the branches from the ground. Many species probably stood up on their back legs. They could reach leaves and fruit above them. Some ground sloths probably had long tongues that could be used to grab food.

Think!

What other animals stand on the ground and reach up into trees? What do they have in common with ground sloths?

Saber-toothed cats were a common predator of giant ground sloths.

Other huge, dangerous animals lived at the same time as ground sloths. Saber-toothed cats and dire wolves might have hunted sloths. Ground sloths were too slow to run away. Instead, they used their powerful claws to fight back. Prehistoric humans also hunted ground sloths for food. They probably worked in groups to fight the sloths with spears.

This image shows different giant ground sloth skeletons at the American Museum of Natural History in New York.

Scientists learn about ground sloths by studying **fossils**. People have been finding giant sloth fossils for hundreds of years. Sometimes they find whole sloth skeletons. Other times, they might find just a footprint. Each fossil gives clues about how ground sloths lived. People can view giant sloth fossils at museums.

Create!

Look online to find pictures of a giant ground sloth skeleton. Then draw a picture of what you think that sloth looked like when it was alive.

GLOSSARY

extinct (ik-STINKT) no longer found living anywhere on Earth

fossils (FAH-suhlz) remains or traces of plants, animals, and other living things that have been preserved as rocks

grazed (GRAYZD) fed on grass and other plants

herbivores (ER-buh-vorz) animals that eat only plants

predators (PREH-duh-tuhrz) animals that hunt other animals for food

species (SPEE-sheez) group of living things that share many characteristics and can mate and produce offspring

FIND OUT MORE

Books

Gleisner, Jenna Lee. *If I Gardened with a Giant Ground Sloth.* Minneapolis, MN: Jump!, 2023.

Neuenfeldt, Elizabeth. *Giant Ground Sloths.* Minneapolis, MN: Bellwether Media, 2025.

Websites

With an adult, learn more online with these suggested searches.

BBC Discover Wildlife: Prehistoric giant ground sloths
Learn more about different ground sloth species and how they became extinct.

La Brea Tar Pits: Walking with Giant Sloths
Take a look at footprints from giant ground sloths that still exist today and find out what scientists learned from them.

INDEX

ABOUT THE AUTHOR

Josh Gregory is the author of more than 250 books for young readers, covering everything from video games and technology to dinosaurs and U.S. history. He lives in Chicago, Illinois.

About Paleoartists

Paleoartists bring the prehistoric world to life! They work with scientists, paleontologists, museums, and their own research to recreate living things from long, long ago. **Mark Witton** is one paleoartist featured in this series. He has been studying prehistoric creatures for over 20 years! **Brian Engh** is another. He builds sculptures, too. He designs and builds whole exhibits. He started Living Relic Productions.